ESSENTIAL ELEMENTS®

POP SONGS

FOR KEYBOARD PERCUSSION

T0086951

The Medallion Calls 2
Game of Thrones 2
The Rainbow Connection 3
The Avengers 3
Hallelujah 4
Kernkraft 400 4
Happy 5
Skyfall 5
Havana 6
High Hopes 6
Señorita 7
Seven Nation Army 7
Heaven 8
Dynamite 8
Counting Stars 9
Sucker 9
Let It Go 10
Wildest Dreams 10
I Gotta Feeling 11
Vida La Vida 11
This Is Me 12
We Are The Champions 12
Blinding Lights 13
Don't Stop Believin' 13
No Time To Die 14
Lead The Way 14
You Will Be Found 15
The Imperial March 15
Believer 16
Angry Birds Theme 16

ISBN 978-1-70515-031-3

HAL•LEONARD®

For all works contained herein:
Unauthorized copying, arranging, adapting, recording, internet posting, public performance, or other distribution of the music in this publication is an infringement of copyright. Infringers are liable under the law.

Visit Hal Leonard Online at
www.halleonard.com

World headquarters, contact:
Hal Leonard
7777 West Bluemound Road
Milwaukee, WI 53213
Email: info@halleonard.com

In Europe, contact:
Hal Leonard Europe Limited
1 Red Place
London, W1K 6PL
Email: info@halleonardeurope.com

In Australia, contact:
Hal Leonard Australia Pty. Ltd.
4 Lentara Court
Cheltenham, Victoria, 3192 Australia
Email: info@halleonard.com.au

THE MEDALLION CALLS

from PIRATES OF THE CARIBBEAN: THE CURSE OF THE BLACK PEARL

Music by KLAUS BADELT

© 2003 Walt Disney Music Company
All Rights Reserved. Used by Permission.

GAME OF THRONES

Theme from the HBO Series GAME OF THRONES

By RAMIN DJAWADI

Copyright © 2011 TL MUSIC PUBLISHING
This arrangement Copyright © 2023 TL MUSIC PUBLISHING
All Rights Administered by UNIVERSAL MUSIC CORP.
All Rights Reserved Used by Permission

THE RAINBOW CONNECTION

from THE MUPPET MOVIE

Words and Music by
PAUL WILLIAMS and KENNETH L. ASCHER

Moderately, with a lilt

© 1979 Fuzzy Muppet Songs
All Rights Reserved. Used by Permission.

THE AVENGERS

from THE AVENGERS

Composed by ALAN SILVESTRI

Moderately, with intensity

© 2012 Marvel Superheroes Music
All Rights Reserved. Used by Permission.

HALLELUJAH

Words and Music by LEONARD COHEN

Copyright © 1985 Sony Music Publishing (US) LLC
This arrangement Copyright © 2023 Sony Music Publishing (US) LLC
All Rights Administered by Sony Music Publishing (US) LLC, 424 Church Street, Suite 1200, Nashville, TN 37219
International Copyright Secured All Rights Reserved

KERNKRAFT 400

By EMANUEL GUENTHER and FLORIAN SENFTER

Copyright © 1999 UKW Publishing Florian Senfter
This arrangement Copyright © 2023 UKW Publishing Florian Senfter
All Rights Administered in the U.S. by Downtown DLJ Songs o/b/o Budde Music Inc.
All Rights Reserved Used by Permission

HAPPY

Words and Music by PHARRELL WILLIAMS

Copyright © 2013 EMI April Music Inc., More Water From Nazareth and Universal Pictures Global Music
This arrangement Copyright © 2023 EMI April Music Inc., More Water From Nazareth and Universal Pictures Global Music
All Rights on behalf of EMI April Music Inc. and More Water From Nazareth Administered by Sony Music Publishing (US) LLC, 424 Church Street, Suite 1200, Nashville, TN 37219
All Rights on behalf of Universal Pictures Global Music Controlled and Administered by Universal Music Works
International Copyright Secured All Rights Reserved

SKYFALL

from the Motion Picture SKYFALL

Words and Music by
ADELE ADKINS and PAUL EPWORTH

Copyright © 2012 MELTED STONE PUBLISHING LTD. and EMI MUSIC PUBLISHING LTD.
This arrangement Copyright © 2023 MELTED STONE PUBLISHING LTD. and EMI MUSIC PUBLISHING LTD.
All Rights for MELTED STONE PUBLISHING LTD. in the U.S. and Canada Controlled and Administered by UNIVERSAL - SONGS OF POLYGRAM INTERNATIONAL, INC.
All Rights for EMI MUSIC PUBLISHING LTD. Administered by SONY MUSIC PUBLISHING (US) LLC, 424 Church Street, Suite 1200, Nashville, TN 37219
All Rights Reserved Used by Permission

HAVANA

Words and Music by CAMILA CABELLO, LOUIS BELL, PHARRELL WILLIAMS,
ADAM FEENEY, ALI TAMPOSI, JEFFERY LAMAR WILLIAMS, BRIAN LEE,
ANDREW WOTMAN, BRITTANY HAZZARD and KAAN GUNESBERK

Copyright © 2017 Maidmetal Limited, Milamoon Songs, Sony Music Publishing (UK), EMI April Music Inc., EMI Pop Music Publishing, More Water From Nazareth,
EMI Blackwood Music Inc., EMI Music Publishing Ltd., Nyankingmusic, Sam Fam Beats, Reservoir 416, Young Stoner Life Publishing LLC, Andrew Watt Music,
These Are Songs Of Pulse, People Over Planes, Warner-Tamerlane Publishing Corp., Songs From The Dong, Atlantic Songs, 300 Rainwater Music and Universal Music Corp.
This arrangement Copyright © 2023 Maidmetal Limited, Milamoon Songs, Sony Music Publishing (UK), EMI April Music Inc., EMI Pop Music Publishing, More Water From Nazareth,
EMI Blackwood Music Inc., EMI Music Publishing Ltd., Nyankingmusic, Sam Fam Beats, Reservoir 416, Young Stoner Life Publishing LLC, Andrew Watt Music,
These Are Songs Of Pulse, People Over Planes, Warner-Tamerlane Publishing Corp., Songs From The Dong, Atlantic Songs, 300 Rainwater Music and Universal Music Corp.
All Rights on behalf of Maidmetal Limited, Milamoon Songs, Sony Music Publishing (UK), EMI April Music Inc., EMI Pop Music Publishing,
More Water From Nazareth, EMI Blackwood Music Inc., EMI Music Publishing Ltd., Nyankingmusic and Sam Fam Beats
Administered by Sony Music Publishing (US) LLC, 424 Church Street, Suite 1200, Nashville, TN 37219
All Rights on behalf of Reservoir 416 and Young Stoner Life Publishing LLC Administered Worldwide by Reservoir Media Management, Inc.
All Rights on behalf of Andrew Watt Music Administered Worldwide by Songs Of Kobalt Music Publishing
All Rights on behalf of These are Songs Of Pulse and People Over Planes Administered by Concord Sounds c/o Concord Music Publishing
All Rights on behalf of Songs From The Dong and Atlantic Songs Administered by Warner-Tamerlane Publishing Corp.
All Rights on behalf of 300 Rainwater Music Administered by Songs Of Universal, Inc.
International Copyright Secured All Rights Reserved

HIGH HOPES

Words and Music by BRENDON URIE, WILLIAM LOBBAN BEAN,
JONAS JEBERG, SAMUEL HOLLANDER, JACOB SINCLAIR,
JENNY OWEN YOUNGS, ILSEY JUBER, LAUREN PRITCHARD and TAYLA PARX

Copyright © 2018 Listen To This Shhh, Songs By Cook Classic, Artist 101 Publishing Group, Kobalt Music Services America, Hipgnosis Side A,
Hipgnosis Beats, Sinclair Empire, Hipgnosis Notes, A Song Can Be About Anything Music, Girls Raised By Wolves,
Sony Music Publishing (US) LLC, Sparko Phone Music and Lolopritch Music, Warner-Tamerlane Publishing Corp. and Taylor Monet Music
Copyright © 2023 Listen To This Shhh, Songs By Cook Classic, Artist 101 Publishing Group, Kobalt Music Services America, Hipgnosis Side A, Hipgnosis Beats, Sinclair Empire, Hipgnosis Notes,
A Song Can Be About Anything Music, Girls Raised By Wolves, Sony Music Publishing (US) LLC, Sparko Phone Musolopritch Music, Warner-Tamerlane Publishing Corp. and Taylor Monet Music
All Rights for Listen To This Shhh Administered Worldwide by Kobalt Songs Music Publishing
All Rights for Songs By Cook Classic and Artist 101 Publishing Group Administered Worldwide by Songs Of Kobalt Music Publishing
All Rights for Hipgnosis Side A, Hipgnosis Beats, Sinclair Empire, Hipgnosis Notes, A Song Can Be About Anything Music and Girls Raised By Wolves Administered by Hipgnosis Songs Group
All Rights for Sony Music Publishing (US) LLC, Sparko Phone Music and Lolopritch Music Administered by Sony Music Publishing (US) LLC, 424 Church Street, Suite 1200, Nashville, TN 37219
All Rights for Taylor Monet Music Administered by Warner-Tamerlane Publishing Corp.
International Copyright Secured All Rights Reserved

SEÑORITA

Words and Music by CAMILA CABELLO,
CHARLOTTE AITCHISON, JACK PATTERSON,
SHAWN MENDES, MAGNUS HOIBERG,
BENJAMIN LEVIN, ALI TAMPOSI
and ANDREW WOTMAN

Copyright © 2019 Maidmetal Limited, Milamoon Songs, Stellar Songs Ltd., EMI Music Publishing Ltd., Songs Of Universal, Inc., Mendes Music, Infinite Stripes,
Back Hair Music Publishing, Universal Music Works, Please Don't Forget To Pay Me Music, Reservoir 416 and Andrew Watt Music
This arrangement Copyright © 2023 Maidmetal Limited, Milamoon Songs, Stellar Songs Ltd., EMI Music Publishing Ltd., Songs Of Universal, Inc., Mendes Music,
Infinite Stripes, Back Hair Music Publishing, Universal Music Works, Please Don't Forget To Pay Me Music, Reservoir 416 and Andrew Watt Music
All Rights on behalf of Maidmetal Limited, Milamoon Songs, Stellar Songs Ltd. and EMI Music Publishing Ltd.
Administered by Sony Music Publishing (US) LLC, 424 Church Street, Suite 1200, Nashville, TN 37219
All Rights on behalf of Mendes Music, Infinite Stripes and Back Hair Music Publishing Administered by Songs Of Universal, Inc.
All Rights on behalf of Please Don't Forget To Pay Me Music Administered by Universal Music Works
All Rights on behalf of Reservoir 416 Administered Worldwide by Reservoir Media Management, Inc.
All Rights on behalf of Andrew Watt Music Administered Worldwide by Songs Of Kobalt Music Publishing
International Copyright Secured All Rights Reserved

SEVEN NATION ARMY

Words and Music by JACK WHITE

Copyright © 2003 SONGS OF UNIVERSAL, INC. and PEPPERMINT STRIPE MUSIC
This arrangement Copyright © 2023 SONGS OF UNIVERSAL, INC. and PEPPERMINT STRIPE MUSIC
All Rights Administered by SONGS OF UNIVERSAL, INC.
All Rights Reserved Used by Permission

HEAVEN

Words and Music by SHY CARTER,
LINDSAY RIMES and MATTHEW MCGINN

Copyright © 2017 BMG Platinum Songs, You Want How Much Of What Publishing, Worldwide EMG Music B,
EMI Blackwood Music Inc., Koala T Tunes, Smackworks Music and Smack Blue LLC
This arrangement Copyright © 2023 BMG Platinum Songs, You Want How Much Of What Publishing, Worldwide EMG Music B,
EMI Blackwood Music Inc., Koala T Tunes, Smackworks Music and Smack Blue LLC
All Rights for BMG Platinum Songs, You Want How Much Of What Publishing and Worldwide EMG Music B Administered by BMG Rights Management (US) LLC
All Rights for EMI Blackwood Music Inc. and Koala T Tunes Administered by Sony Music Publishing (US) LLC, 424 Church Street, Suite 1200, Nashville, TN 37219
All Rights for Smackworks Music and Smack Blue LLC Administered Worldwide by Kobalt Group Publishing
All Rights Reserved Used by Permission

DYNAMITE

Words and Music by
JESSICA AGOMBAR and DAVID STEWART

Copyright © 2020 Stellar Songs Limited
This arrangement Copyright © 2023 Stellar Songs Limited
All Rights Administered by Sony Music Publishing (US) LLC, 424 Church Street, Suite 1200, Nashville, TN 37219
International Copyright Secured All Rights Reserved

COUNTING STARS

Words and Music by RYAN TEDDER

Copyright © 2013 Sony Music Publishing (US) LLC, Velvet Hammer Music and Midnite Miracle Music
This arrangement Copyright © 2023 Sony Music Publishing (US) LLC, Velvet Hammer Music and Midnite Miracle Music
All Rights Administered by Sony Music Publishing (US) LLC, 424 Church Street, Suite 1200, Nashville, TN 37219
International Copyright Secured All Rights Reserved

SUCKER

Words and Music by NICK JONAS, JOSEPH JONAS, MILES ALE, MUSTAFA AHMED, RYAN TEDDER, LOUIS BELL, ADAM FEENEY, KEVIN JONAS and HOMER STEINWEISS

Copyright © 2019 SONGS OF UNIVERSAL, INC., NICK JONAS PUBLISHING, JOSEPH JONAS PUBLISHING, ELECTRIC FEEL MUSIC, WRITE ME A SONG PUBLISHING, EMI MUSIC PUBLISHING LTD., MYNY MUSIC, SAM FAM BEATS, EMI APRIL MUSIC INC., PAUL KEVIN JONAS II PUBLISHING and BMG PLATINUM SONGS US
This arrangement Copyright © 2023 SONGS OF UNIVERSAL, INC., NICK JONAS PUBLISHING, JOSEPH JONAS PUBLISHING, ELECTRIC FEEL MUSIC, WRITE ME A SONG PUBLISHING, EMI MUSIC PUBLISHING LTD., MYNY MUSIC, SAM FAM BEATS, EMI APRIL MUSIC INC., PAUL KEVIN JONAS II PUBLISHING and BMG PLATINUM SONGS US
All Rights for NICK JONAS PUBLISHING, JOSEPH JONAS PUBLISHING and ELECTRIC FEEL MUSIC Administered by SONGS OF UNIVERSAL, INC.
All Rights for WRITE ME A SONG PUBLISHING Administered by DOWNTOWN GLOBAL TWO
All Rights for EMI MUSIC PUBLISHING LTD., MYNY MUSIC, SAM FAM BEATS, EMI APRIL MUSIC INC. and PAUL KEVIN JONAS II PUBLISHING
Administered by SONY MUSIC PUBLISHING (US) LLC, 424 Church Street, Suite 1200, Nashville, TN 37219
All Rights for BMG PLATINUM SONGS US Administered by BMG RIGHTS MANAGEMENT (US) LLC
All Rights Reserved Used by Permission

LET IT GO

from FROZEN

Music and Lyrics by
KRISTEN ANDERSON-LOPEZ and ROBERT LOPEZ

Half-Time Feel, Mysterious

© 2013 Wonderland Music Company, Inc.
All Rights Reserved. Used by Permission.

WILDEST DREAMS

Words and Music by TAYLOR SWIFT,
MAX MARTIN and SHELLBACK

Moderately Fast

Copyright © 2014 SONGS OF UNIVERSAL, INC., TAYLOR SWIFT MUSIC, SONY MUSIC PUBLISHING (US) LLC, MXM and KMR MUSIC ROYALTIES II SCSP
This arrangement Copyright © 2023 SONGS OF UNIVERSAL, INC., TAYLOR SWIFT MUSIC, SONY MUSIC PUBLISHING (US) LLC, MXM and KMR MUSIC ROYALTIES II SCSP
All Rights for TAYLOR SWIFT MUSIC Administered by SONGS OF UNIVERSAL, INC.
All Rights for SONY MUSIC PUBLISHING (US) LLC Administered by SONY MUSIC PUBLISHING (US) LLC, 424 Church Street, Suite 1200, Nashville, TN 37219
All Rights for MXM and KMR MUSIC ROYALTIES II SCSP Administered Worldwide by KOBALT SONGS MUSIC PUBLISHING
All Rights Reserved Used by Permission

I GOTTA FEELING

Words and Music by WILL ADAMS,
ALLAN PINEDA, JAIME GOMEZ, STACY FERGUSON,
DAVID GUETTA and FREDERIC RIESTERER

Copyright © 2009 BMG Sapphire Songs, I Am Composing LLC, BMG Platinum Songs US, Apl de Ap Publishing LLC,
Tab Magnetic Publishing, Headphone Junkie Publishing LLC, What A Publishing Ltd., KMR Music Royalties II SCSp, Shapiro, Bernstein & Co. Inc. and Rister Editions
This arrangement Copyright © 2023 BMG Sapphire Songs, I Am Composing LLC, BMG Platinum Songs US, Apl de Ap Publishing LLC, Tab Magnetic Publishing,
Headphone Junkie Publishing LLC, What A Publishing Ltd., KMR Music Royalties II SCSp, Shapiro, Bernstein & Co. Inc. and Rister Editions
All Rights for BMG Sapphire Songs, I Am Composing LLC, BMG Platinum Songs US, Apl de Ap Publishing LLC,
Tab Magnetic Publishing and Headphone Junkie Publishing LLC Administered by BMG Rights Management (US) LLC
All Rights for What A Publishing Ltd. and KMR Music Royalties II SCSp Administered Worldwide by Kobalt Music Group Ltd.
All Rights for Shapiro, Bernstein & Co. Inc. and Rister Editions in the United States, Ireland and the United Kingdom Administered by Reservoir Media Management, Inc.
All Rights Reserved Used by Permission

VIDA LA VIDA

Words and Music by
GUY BERRYMAN, JON BUCKLAND
WILL CHAMPION and CHRIS MARTIN

Copyright © 2008 by Universal Music Publishing MGB Ltd.
This arrangement Copyright © 2023 by Universal Music Publishing MGB Ltd.
All Rights in the United States and Canada Administered by Universal Music - MGB Songs
International Copyright Secured All Rights Reserved

THIS IS ME

from THE GREATEST SHOWMAN

Words and Music by
BENJ PASEK and JUSTIN PAUL

With Emotion

Copyright © 2017 Breathelike Music, Pick In A Pinch Music and T C F Music Publishing, Inc.
This arrangement Copyright © 2023 Breathelike Music, Pick In A Pinch Music and T C F Music Publishing, Inc.
All Rights for Breathelike Music and Pick In A Pinch Music Administered Worldwide by Kobalt Songs Music Publishing
All Rights Reserved Used by Permission

WE ARE THE CHAMPIONS

Words and Music by
FREDDIE MERCURY

Moderately Slow

Copyright © 1977 Queen Music Ltd.
Copyright Renewed
This arrangement Copyright © 2023 Queen Music Ltd.
All Rights Administered by Sony Music Publishing (US) LLC, 424 Church Street, Suite 1200, Nashville, TN 37219
International Copyright Secured All Rights Reserved

BLINDING LIGHTS

Words and Music by ABEL TESFAYE,
MAX MARTIN, JASON QUENNEVILLE,
OSCAR HOLTER and AHMAD BALSHE

Fast, Driving Retro Pop

Copyright © 2019 KMR Music Royalties II SCSp, MXM, Universal Music Corp., Sal And Co LP, WC Music Corp. and Songs Of Wolf Cousins
This arrangement Copyright © 2023 KMR Music Royalties II SCSp, MXM, Universal Music Corp., Sal And Co LP, WC Music Corp. and Songs Of Wolf Cousins
All Rights for KMR Music Royalties II SCSp and MXM Administered Worldwide by Kobalt Songs Music Publishing
All Rights for Sal And Co LP Administered by Universal Music Corp.
All Rights for Songs Of Wolf Cousins Administered by WC Music Corp.
All Rights Reserved Used by Permission

DON'T STOP BELIEVIN'

Words and Music by STEVE PERRY,
NEAL SCHON and JONATHAN CAIN

Moderate Rock

Copyright © 1981 Lacey Boulevard Music (BMI) and Weed-High Nightmare Music (BMI)
This arrangement Copyright © 2023 Lacey Boulevard Music (BMI) and Weed-High Nightmare Music (BMI)
All Rights for Weed-High Nightmare Music Administered by Wixen Music Publishing Inc.
International Copyright Secured All Rights Reserved

NO TIME TO DIE

from NO TIME TO DIE

Words and Music by BILLIE EILISH O'CONNELL
and FINNEAS O'CONNELL

Copyright © 2020 UNIVERSAL MUSIC CORP., DRUP, U/A MUSIC, INC. and LAST FRONTIER
This arrangement Copyright © 2023 UNIVERSAL MUSIC CORP., DRUP, U/A MUSIC, INC. and LAST FRONTIER
All Rights for DRUP and U/A MUSIC, INC. Administered by UNIVERSAL MUSIC CORP.
All Rights for LAST FRONTIER Administered Worldwide by KOBALT SONGS MUSIC PUBLISHING
All Rights Reserved Used by Permission

LEAD THE WAY

from RAYA AND THE LAST DRAGON

Music and Lyrics by JHENE AIKO

© 2021 Wonderland Music Company, Inc.
All Rights Reserved. Used by Permission.

YOU WILL BE FOUND

from DEAR EVAN HANSEN

Music and Lyrics by
BENJ PASEK and JUSTIN PAUL

Copyright © 2017 Pick In A Pinch Music (ASCAP) and Breathelike Music (ASCAP)
This arrangement Copyright © 2023 Pick In A Pinch Music (ASCAP) and Breathelike Music (ASCAP)
All Rights Administered by Kobalt Songs Music Publishing
All Rights Reserved Used by Permission

THE IMPERIAL MARCH (Darth Vader's Theme)

from STAR WARS: THE EMPIRE STRIKES BACK

Music by JOHN WILLIAMS

© 1980 Bantha Music and Warner-Tamerlane Publishing Corp.
All Rights Reserved. Used by Permission.

BELIEVER

Words and Music by DAN REYNOLDS, WAYNE SERMON, BEN MCKEE, DANIEL PLATZMAN, JUSTIN TRANTOR, MATTIAS LARSSON and ROBIN FREDRICKSSON

Copyright © 2017 SONGS OF UNIVERSAL, INC., SONGS FOR KIDINAKORNER, IMAGINE DRAGONS PUBLISHING, WARNER-TAMERLANE PUBLISHING CORP., JUSTIN'S SCHOOL FOR GIRLS, WOLF COUSINS, MA-JAY PUBLISHING and WARNER CHAPPELL MUSIC SCANDINAVIA AB
This arrangement Copyright © 2023 SONGS OF UNIVERSAL, INC., SONGS FOR KIDINAKORNER, IMAGINE DRAGONS PUBLISHING, WARNER-TAMERLANE PUBLISHING CORP., JUSTIN'S SCHOOL FOR GIRLS, WOLF COUSINS, MA-JAY PUBLISHING and WARNER CHAPPELL MUSIC SCANDINAVIA AB
All Rights for SONGS FOR KIDINAKORNER and IMAGINE DRAGONS PUBLISHING Administered by SONGS OF UNIVERSAL, INC.
All Rights for JUSTIN'S SCHOOL FOR GIRLS Administered by WARNER-TAMERLANE PUBLISHING CORP.
All Rights for WOLF COUSINS, MA-JAY PUBLISHING and WARNER CHAPPELL MUSIC SCANDINAVIA AB in the U.S. and Canada Administered by WC MUSIC CORP.
All Rights Reserved Used by Permission

ANGRY BIRDS THEME

By ARI PULKKINEN

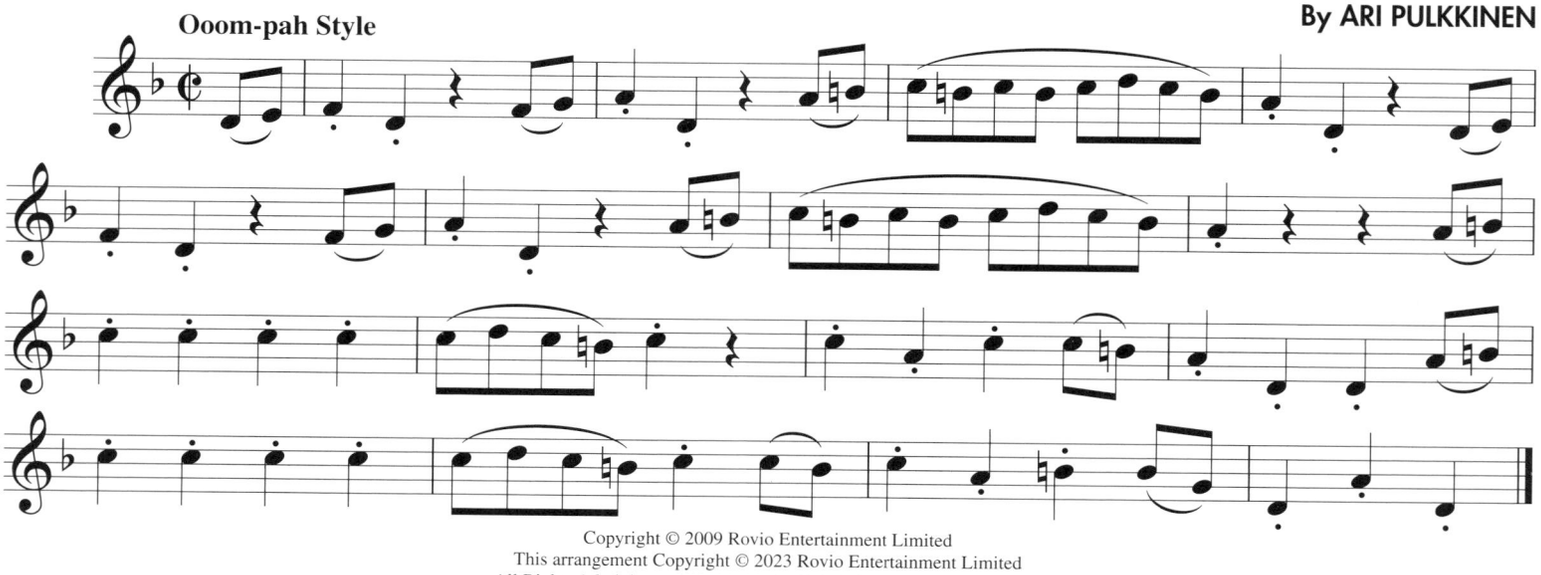

Copyright © 2009 Rovio Entertainment Limited
This arrangement Copyright © 2023 Rovio Entertainment Limited
All Rights Administered Worldwide by Kobalt Songs Music Publishing
All Rights Reserved Used by Permission